WINNING AT HUMAN RELATIONS

How to Keep from Victimizing Yourself

Elwood N. Chapman

A FIFTY-MINUTE™ SERIES BOOK

CRISP PUBLICATIONS, INC.
Menlo Park, California

WINNING AT HUMAN RELATIONS
How to Keep from Victimizing Yourself

Elwood N. Chapman

CREDITS
Editor: **Michael Crisp**
Designer: **Carol Harris**
Typesetting: **Interface Studio**
Cover Design: **Carol Harris**
Artwork: **Ralph Mapson**

Copyright © 1989 by Crisp Publications, Inc.
Printed in the United States of America

Distribution to the U.S. Trade:

National Book Network, Inc.
4720 Boston Way
Lanham, MD 20706
1-800-462-6420

Library of Congress Catalog Card Number 88-63804
Chapman, Elwood N.
Winning At Human Relations
ISBN 0-931961-86-6

This book is printed on recyclable paper with soy ink.

ABOUT THIS BOOK

WINNING AT HUMAN RELATIONS is not like most books. It has a unique "self-paced" format that encourages a reader to become personally involved. Designed to be "read with a pencil," there are an abundance of exercises, activities, assessments and cases that invite participation.

The objective of WINNING AT HUMAN RELATIONS is to provide guidelines which will help a reader understand the importance of developing and maintaining positive human relations both at work and at home.

WINNING AT HUMAN RELATIONS (and the other self-improvement titles listed on the order form in the back of this book) can be used effectively in a number of ways. Here are some possibilities:

—**Individual Study.** Because the book is self-instructional, all that is needed is a quiet place, some time and a pencil. By completing the activities and exercises, a reader will not only receive valuable feedback, but also practical steps for self-improvement.

—**Workshops and Seminars.** This book is ideal for assigned reading prior to a workshop or seminar. With the basics in hand, the quality of the participation will improve and more time can be spent on concept extentions and applications during the program. The book is also effective when it is distributed at the beginning of a session, and participants "work through" the contents.

—**Remote Location Training.** Books can be sent to those not able to attend "home office" training sessions.

There are many other possibilities that depend on the objectives, program or ideas of the user.

One thing for sure. Even after this book has been read, it will be looked at—and thought about—again and again.

AUTHOR'S NOTE

Organizations pay a monumental price in lost productivity because of emotional disturbances and negative attitudes caused by damaged interpersonal relationships. A conflict between employees (especially at the executive level) can not only impact the decision-making process, but also sometimes destroy the morale of an entire organization.

In areas where solid customer relations are essential, human relation conflicts can damage or destroy key client relationships. Human conflicts are also a primary cause of employee turnover. With recruitment, employment, and training costs as high as they are, this factor alone can drain the resources of any firm.

Employees lower their personal productivity (and that of their co-workers) when they bring their outside personal conflicts to work with them.

Obviously, those who understand and practice positive human relations skills contribute not only to their organizations but also to their personal career progress. The objective of this book is to help readers build and maintain positive human relationships.

Three excellent additional books dealing with this subject are available using the form in the back of this book. Consider reading: *Attitude: Your Most Priceless Possession; New Employee Orientation* and *Managing Disagreement Constructively*.

PREFACE

The relationships you create and maintain with others, whether in your career or personal world, should be viewed as treasures. They are the jewels of living. When relationships are healthy, open, fun, and mutually rewarding they can enrich your life far beyond material possessions. Good relationships will sustain you in hard times.

But interpersonal human dealings are fragile and demand tender loving care. Even when they seem strong, they can never be taken for granted. Those who become skillful at creating and maintaining on-going positive relationships enjoy more successful careers and happier personal lives. We sometimes refer to these individuals as being ''human relations smart.''

The primary purpose of this book is to assist readers in building and maintaining strong, healthy relationships that will enhance their careers. A secondary purpose is to help readers from becoming primary victims when relationships deteriorate.

Although the emphasis is on career or working relationships, all ideas, principles, and techniques can be applied to one's personal life. Good luck as you learn to ''win at human relations.''

Elwood N. Chapman

CONTENTS

CONTENTS (Continued)

PART I

THE IMPORTANCE
OF
HUMAN RELATIONS
SKILLS

Careers Are Built On Human Relations Skills

"It is human nature to think wisely and act foolishly."

Anatole France

MOST EMPLOYEES UNDERESTIMATE HUMAN RELATIONS

More careers have been damaged through faulty human relations skills than through a lack of technical ability. Many people are technically smart, but human relations dumb, because they seem unaware that simply knowing *how to do a job is not the key to success*. To produce results, most of us depend on others and this requires knowing *how to work with people*. Before this can be done successfully there are many human relations skills to be learned and practiced.

Some individuals underestimate the problems that poor human relations can get them into. They persist in concentrating on personal productivity and ignore the fact that they are part of a complicated ''team'' structure which can only operate efficiently when human relationships are given proper attention.

To be human relations smart it is essential to maintain cooperative relationships with all members of an organization, from co-workers to superiors. Communication must be open and healthy. The quality of any relationship will influence the productivity from that individual.

> When Jessica got her first office job she concentrated almost all of her attention on the accuracy and quantity of her work. Soon her productivity level was higher than any of her six co-workers and she made no secret of it to others. Did Jessica receive a compliment from her supervisior? Yes, but along with it, she was firmly reminded that she was part of a team and ''broadcasting'' her output was causing resentment and hurting the productivity of the others.

Despite the excellent skills Jessica demonstrated; she had not learned to balance her technical competencies with good human relations. She had not learned that her dedicated efforts to achieve personal goals could have a negative impact on the productivity of others. She was blind to the ''big picture'' that involves building and maintaining good relationships with both co-workers and superiors.

HUMAN RELATIONS PRE-TEST

HUMAN RELATIONS PRE-TEST

Although human relations skills are not as easy to identify or quantify as technical skills, they are extremely important to your career progress. The more you practice positive human relations, the less co-workers and superiors will misinterpret your goals and the more supportive they will be.

Twenty human relations competencies are listed below. *Check only those you practice on a daily basis.* The exercise will demonstrate why it is difficult to be considered ''human relations smart.''

I consistently:

☐ Deal with all people in an honest, ethical, and moral way.

☐ Remain positive and upbeat even while working with others who may be negative.

☐ Send out positive verbal and nonverbal signals in all human interactions, including the telephone.

☐ Refuse to be involved in any activity that might victimize another person.

☐ Build and maintain open and healthy working relationships with everyone in the work place. I refuse to play favorites.

☐ Treat everyone, regardless of ethnic or socioeconomic differences with respect.

☐ Work effectively with others regardless of their sexual orientation.

☐ Permit others to restore a damaged relationship with me. I don't hold a grudge.

☐ Maintain a strong relationship with my immediate superior without alienating co-workers.

☐ Am a better than average producer while contributing to the productivity of co-workers.

☐ Refuse to initiate or circulate potentially harmful rumors.

☐ Maintain a good attendance record, including being on time to work.

☐ Show I can live up to my productivity potential without alienating co-workers who do not live up to theirs.

☐ Acknowledge mistakes or misjudgements rather than hiding them.

☐ Refuse to allow small gripes to grow into major upsets.

☐ Am an excellent listener.

☐ Keep a good balance between my home and career lives so that neither suffers.

☐ Look for, and appreciate the good characteristics of others.

☐ Keep my business and personal relationships sufficiently separated.

☐ Make only positive comments about those not present.

SCORE ☐

(Add five points for each square checked.)

A score of 70 or above indicates you are practicing a substantial number of recognized human relations skills; a score of under 50 suggests a review of current practices may be in order.

THE NATURE OF HUMAN RELATIONSHIPS

The most objective way to view human interaction is to concentrate on the relationship itself (consider it to be a conduit or connection between people) and try to forget the personalities on either end. When you focus on the relationship and not worry about the personalities, you can be more objective.

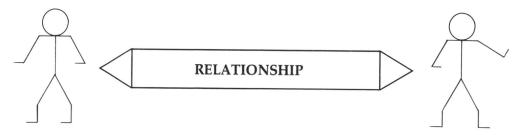

Some people find this impossible to do. As a result, they are unable to ever get beyond personality traits they consider irritating. Result? A personality conflict often develops and the productivity of both parties and those surrounding them is unnecessarily damaged.

Although relationships usually reflect the personalities at each end of the"line," by concentrating on the relationship itself will help one ignore irritating mannerisms and concentrate instead on the potential productivity of the interaction. This concentration on the relationship instead of personalities also helps some people minimize age or value differences, ethnic backgrounds or sexual orientation. Too often these factors negatively affect an individual's ability to see the "bigger picture." When one is able to push such matters aside and deal exclusively with the relationship itself, greater objectivity and fairness will result and things move in a more positive direction.

It is a difficult lesson to learn but if a person allows the personality of another to irritate him or her into a negative attitude, it is that individual who suffers. Away from work, if one wishes to base a personal relationship on personality that is expected. In the workplace, however, where productivity hinges on positive relationships, it can be a different matter.

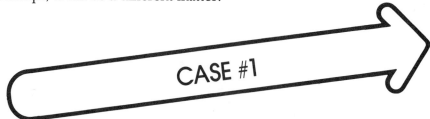

CASE #1

CASE # 1

JEFF AND HIS BOSS

Jeff had invested almost twenty years with a growing, progressive firm. He was proud of his Vice-Presidency, excellent salary, and strong benefits. Recently, Jeff had permitted himself to fall into an intense personality conflict with a new boss. Jeff no longer looked forward to his work and his wife Nancy was increasingly concerned about her husband's emotional health. As a result, she persuaded Jeff to seek professional counseling.

The counselor suggested that Jeff could make progress solving his problem by shifting the focus away from the demanding personality of his boss toward the working relationship between them. Jeff got the message. Later, he and Nancy decided it would help to list the most irritating characteristics of his boss on a piece of paper and then burn it in the fireplace. They reasoned by doing so, Jeff could concentrate on his productivity and not worry about being frustrated by his boss's behavior. Jeff said to himself: "Why allow the strange personality of my boss to affect *my* work and career?"

What chance do you give the strategy of working?

Excellent chance ☐

No chance ☐

Worth trying ☐

To compare your response to that of the author, turn to page 68.

ATTITUDE AND HUMAN RELATIONS

In the work environment, as in your personal life, nothing contributes more to building and maintaining healthy relationships than a positive attitude.

What is a positive attitude?

On the surface, attitude is the way you communicate your mood to others. When you are optimistic and anticipate successful encounters, you transmit a positive attitude. Normally, your co-workers usually respond favorably. When you are pessimistic and expect the worst, your attitude often is negative. When this happens, your fellow employees often avoid you or react negatively to your behavior. Inside your head, where it all starts, attitude is a mind set. It is the way you look at things mentally.

On your way to work, think of attitude as the mental focus you have toward the day ahead. Like using a camera, you can focus your mind either on the positive or negative factors that exist. You can view your work station as an interesting place where you can grow, learn, accomplish career goals, and have some fun; or it can be a drag from the time you arrive until you leave. Perception—the complicated process of viewing and interpreting your environment—is a mental phenomenon. It is within your power to concentrate on selected aspects of your work environment and ignore others. Quite simply, you take the picture of your job and career you want to take.

Why does attitude make such a big difference?

A positive attitude will accomplish three basic goals. (1) It will trigger your enthusiasm toward your work and the people surrounding you. (2) It will enhance your creativity and put you in a position to increase your productivity. (3) And, it will help you make the most of your personality. Co-workers will find it easier to build a relationship with you and they will be motivated to keep it healthy and alive longer.

But as important as attitude may be, it is the *combination* of attitude and solid human relations skills that spell career success.

---

*For more insight into the importance of attitude and human relations see ATTITUDE: YOUR MOST PRICELESS POSSESSION by Elwood N. Chapman at the back of the book.

WORK ATTITUDE SCALE

This exercise is designed to help you measure whether or not you are making a strong effort to achieve the best possible work attitude. If you circle a 10 you are saying you make the supreme effort each day; if you circle a 1, you are saying you have given up on making any attitude improvement in this area. Be honest.

		HIGH (Positive)					LOW (Negative)			

1. I concentrate on adjusting my attitude each morning on the way to work 10 9 8 7 6 5 4 3 2 1

2. If I were to guess, I believe my boss would rate my attitude as a 10 9 8 7 6 5 4 3 2 1

3. I make a serious effort each day to build positive working relationships with all my co-workers 10 9 8 7 6 5 4 3 2 1

4. I believe my co-workers would rate my current attitude as a 10 9 8 7 6 5 4 3 2 1

5. If there were a meter that could gauge my sense of humor in the workplace, it would read close to a 10 9 8 7 6 5 4 3 2 1

6. I rate my enthusiasm toward my current job as a 10 9 8 7 6 5 4 3 2 1

7. I never permit little things to negatively influence my positive attitude 10 9 8 7 6 5 4 3 2 1

8. I would rate the attitude I communicate over the telephone as a 10 9 8 7 6 5 4 3 2 1

9. The patience and sensitivity I show to others (inside or outside of any organization) deserves a rating of 10 9 8 7 6 5 4 3 2 1

10. Based upon my work performance and general attitude, I deserve a 10 9 8 7 6 5 4 3 2 1

TOTAL _____

A score of 90 or over is a signal that you are doing an outstanding job in human relations. A score between 70 and 90 indicates that your attitude is good and you demonstrate you are human relations smart. A rating between 50 and 70 suggests an improvement in your attitude would measurably improve your working relationships. If you rated yourself below 50, your human relations progress is being severely restricted by your attitude.

PRODUCTIVITY AND HUMAN RELATIONS

In any team situation, every person is expected to carry a fair share of the work load. Managers have the responsibility of evaluating the individual contribution of team members. It is natural for some individuals to carry a slightly heavier load because of ability, experience, motivation or pride. Small productivity imbalances are no problem. But when a gap becomes noticeably excessive, team relationships often deteriorate.

Sometimes high producers become emotionally disturbed over the low productivity of others. As a result, high producers may "sound off" and lose the support of other team members or allow their own productivity to suffer. Result? Departmental productivity drops.

When John started his teaching career his standards were so high that he permitted himself to become upset with colleagues who had measurably lower standards. After one year in the classroom he left for another career. Today he looks back and realizes that he would have been happier to remain in teaching. He freely acknowledges he permitted the behavior of others to chase him away from the career he really wanted.

For most employees, the solution to working with those who perform at lower levels is a three step process. (1) Continue to set a good example and do your level best to ignore the personal productivity of others. This is difficult because it may drag on indefinitely. (2) It may be possible to resolve the problem through the use of conflict resolution techniques such as mutual understanding, bargaining, or collaboration of some kind. (3) It could be necessary to take the situation to a superior in the hope she or he is capable of resolving the imbalance. Ultimately a solution is necessary or the high producers (those management needs to keep) may leave. These individuals may rightfully perceive that under certain conditions leaving is the best available choice.

BALANCE RELATIONSHIP BUILDING IN FAVOR OF CO-WORKERS

Your most important working relationship is with your immediate superior. In most cases, the best way to maintain an excellent relationship with your boss is to concentrate on improving relationships with your co-workers.

Why is this so?

Perceptive supervisors observe your ability to work well with co-workers because positive working relationships impact productivity. When superiors notice you are able to build good relationships with team members, you automatically build good relationships with them.

> When Jill started her new career with Mytech she was friendly, open and not the least bit intimidated by superiors. Jill devoted most of her relationship-building time with her co-workers. Result? Her superiors were impressed with her human skills and the contribution she made to other members of the team. It paid off a year later when Jill was promoted to a supervisory role at another location.

The fact that Jill concentrated on co-worker relationships does not mean she neglected others. She did everything possible to maintain excellent relations with her immediate supervisor. She kept him informed and always made sure she provided follow-through on her projects. She was smart enough to know that any moves she made which might lead to favoritism from above could backfire. She simply let her skills at building positive relationships with others speak for her.

JILL

COMMUNICATIONS IS THE LIFE BLOOD OF ALL RELATIONSHIPS

Verbal communication between two people is usually the way an important relationship gets started.

> The twenty year relationship between Brooke and Laura started when they found themselves in the same management training program. Sharing experiences at the end of each day, they built a common bond that has lasted for many years.

Regular communication (face to face, telephone, and written) is almost always necessary to maintain a relationship over an extended period of time.

> Within a year Brooke took her talents to another firm. She and Laura continued to maintain their relationship through frequent telephone calls and meeting for dinner at least once a month. The bond between them strengthened as they provided mutual support and career enhancement strategies to each other.

Immediate, open, face to face communication is the best way to restore a damaged relationship.

> At one point, they had a falling out caused by Brooke rejoining Laura's company and being supervised by Laura. Brooke was not prepared for the more authoritative leadership style that Laura had developed since the "old days." It became necessary for Laura to initiate a one-on-one meeting where the problem was openly discussed. Thanks to sensitivity and mutual respect from both ends, their personal relationship became close again despite the new manager-employee situation.

When it came to Laura and Brooke, they were human relations smart because they learned to communicate, communicate, communicate! Like a delicate plant that is nutured to maturity through water, fertilizer, and tender, loving care, human relationships are nutured through communication. The next time you hear of a relationship that has fallen apart, it is safe to assume that a lack of communication played an important role in the separation.

THE MUTUAL REWARD THEORY

It is usually easy to initiate positive relationships in the workplace. The challenge comes in building and maintaining these relationships to the benefit of all concerned. One way to help this happen, is to see that each individual receives rewards from the other party that are approximately equal in value. This simple ''reward exchange'' policy is the basis for The Mutual Reward Theory.

The Mutual Reward Theory (MRT) states that for a relationship to remain healthy, both parties must benefit. That is, there needs to be a voluntary, essentially equal exchange of benefits between the two parties. The rewards need not be the same in kind or number, but when one person starts to receive more than he or she gives, the relationship is vulnerable.

George, new on the job, and Herb with ten years seniority, started out with a promising working relationship. George, a recent graduate with excellent computer skills was always willing to leave his work station and help Herb with his specialized computer applications. Herb, in turn, willingly provided George with insights on how to better understand the corporate culture. The relationship was mutually rewarding. Both came out ahead. If, however, either party started to do more ''taking'' than ''giving'' the relationship could begin to deteriorate.

For any relationship to remain healthy, both parties must appreciate the mutual exchange of benefits. It is therefore human relations smart to make sure that the ''other party'' in any important relationship continues to receive appropriate rewards. In the above situation, if George withdrew his computer support, a possible solution might be for Herb to sit down with George and work out another ''reward mix.''

THE INSENSITIVITY OF OTHERS CAN CAUSE DAMAGE TO YOUR RELATIONSHIPS

The way others treat you can cause you to react emotionally and damage an important relationship. Sometimes the other party may not realize her or his behavior is upsetting you. As a result, you may harm yourself if you are over-sensitive to the incident.

How often have you heard the expression ''I can take (name of person) or leave him or her?'' This usually means the individual making the statement has been offended and is backing away from a relationship with that person.

To help you avoid over-reacting, prioritize the items listed below. Write a #1 opposite the incident that would most upset you to a #6 for the one that would upset you least.

I become upset when another person:

☐ Seems to ignore me at a gathering where others are present.

☐ Fails to keep what I believe was a promise.

☐ Holds back on information I feel I deserve to know.

☐ Cancels an appointment.

☐ Refuses to be a good listener.

☐ Pays more attention to another person.

If a working relationship is important, do not permit it to be damaged because of situations similar to those listed above. Otherwise your career may suffer while the offending party walks away unknowing of the damage that has been caused. Most of us have permitted an important relationship to deteriorate over a minor matter that was unintended by the other party. The best way to handle situations like those mentioned is to either give the other person the benefit of the doubt, or discuss the matter openly and ''clear the air.''

Which will be your future strategy?

I intend to say nothing if a situation similar to those listed occurs. I will however, be more tolerant and give the other party the benefit of the doubt. This means I will quickly forgive and forget.   Check here. ☐

I plan to discuss potential misinterpretations immediately to clear the air and restore the relationship as quickly as possible. Talking it over will help improve communications.   Check here. ☐

ABSENTEEISM AND TARDINESS DAMAGES RELATIONSHIPS

One of the most frequent ways employees damage their relationships is through needless tardiness and absenteeism. Here's why.

1. A poor attendance record builds a credibility gap with superiors.

2. Frequent absence from responsibilities causes co-workers to pick up the slack.

3. Records that reflect heavy absenteeism and lateness are permanent and can be evaluated by other managers reviewing internal candidates for promotion.

4. In case of layoffs, cutbacks, or reassignments, those with poor records are often the first to go.

Despite the penalties listed above, many capable employees fail to see how they damage relationships in all directions.

> Rebecca was, without question, the most capable technician on the team. When she was on the job and on top of things her productivity was exceptional. But Rebecca was frequently late and periodically absent. This caused other team members problems because they had to adjust their work loads to offset Rebecca's lack of dependability.
>
> Ultimately Rebecca's career was permanently damaged because of on-going absenteeism. When asked about it she replied: "I took a chance and lost. I didn't have to be late or absent, I just thought that I was good enough to get by with it. When my co-workers got tired of holding me up, the game was over."

For some strange reason, many otherwise clever people fail to see the human relations aspects of being tardy or absent. By refusing to discipline themselves, their credibility is in question even when they have legitimate reasons for being late or away from work.

RELATIONSHIP REWARD—CONFLICT CHART

One way to create conflict within a relationship is to fail to provide the expected behavior to the party at the other end of the line. The column on the left lists some behaviors/rewards that *maintain* a relationship. The column on the right demonstrates that when the same rewards are *not* provided they become "conflict points." Feel free to add your own.

REWARDS	CONFLICT POINTS
Free and open communication	Unwilling or poor communication
Accepting value differences	Prejudice
Carrying full load	Failure to pull your expected weight
Balanced rewards	Unequal reward system
Trust	Lack of trust
Recognizing the independence of another	Jealousy
Sense of humor	Lack of humor
Sensitive to needs	Insensitive to needs
Generous (with time, talent, money, etc.)	Stingy beyond reason
Keeps other informed	Failure to inform
High on patience	Low on patience
Keeps promises	Forgets promises
Seldom absent	Frequently absent
Excellent follow-through	Little follow-through
Handles own personal problems	Unloads on co-workers
Remains upbeat	Consistantly negative
_____	_____
_____	_____

Those who provide co-workers (and friends) with a good and consistent reward mix will maintain excellent relationships. Those who fail to do so create "conflict points" that damage relationships.

CASE # 2	# JENNIFER'S IMAGE

Jennifer, an experienced professional office worker, was immediately impressed with Vickie when she joined the department. Jennifer went out of her way to help Vickie feel comfortable in her new environment. As a result, Vickie introduced Jennifer to social friends away from work. Soon they were enjoying evenings out together and wound up sharing an apartment. It appeared, on the surface, to be a mutually rewarding arrangement. But, after a few months, it became apparent that Vickie did not have a genuine interest in her job. Her productivity never improved and required substantial co-worker support.

Soon, to the surprise of others, Jennifer started making excuses for her friend. Although Jennifer had an excellent image and was considered management material before Vickie arrived, she was now viewed as a person with questionable judgement. Without being fully aware of what was happening, Jennifer became a victim in what had started to be a legitimate mutually rewarding relationship. Looking back later Jennifer made these comments:

> ''I made a serious human relations mistake. My need to be more socially accepted and have a good time blinded me. In time, it became obvious that Vickie was hanging on to my work coattails and I was hanging on to her social coattails. Our reward system got out of line when she traded on my personal productivity and status to keep her job. When things got so bad that Vickie was terminated, I had to rebuild my image with co-workers and management. It won't happen again.''

Would it have been possible for Jennifer to maintain her professional status and still keep an outside relationship with Vickie? Why did it take Jennifer so long to realize what was happening? See authors response on page 68.

WHEN YOUR CAREER SEEMS "ON HOLD"

In each career path there are periods when an individual must "stand still" as far as upward mobility is concerned. There may be promotions in the future, but for now the organization can do nothing. This is known as a "plateau period."

Such a period must be understood, because it has the potential to turn a person negative. This can cause the individual to neglect his or her human relations opportunities.

> Due to slower than expected growth and some restructuring, management was aware that it would be a tough waiting period for Cecil and Chavez. Both were counseled to be patient and continue to prepare for promotions that should eventually materialize. Chavez took these suggestions seriously and used the waiting period to improve relationships and upgrade his competencies. Cecil, on the other hand, became discouraged and let things slip. When the environment improved, Chavez was promoted, but Cecil was not ready. In talking it over with the Director of Human Resources Cecil was told: "When you failed to stay positive, maintain relationships, and keep your personal productivity high, you disqualified yourself."

Plateau periods are never easy. It is difficult to keep learning and stay positive when you feel you are ready for more responsibility but nothing happens. Some occasions might call for activating a Plan B (see page 62). But for those who remain with the organization and want to progress, staying interested and involved is necessary to avoid career damage.

Stay focused during plateau periods

TURNING A FAMILY PROBLEM INTO A CAREER ADVANTAGE

Jack Smith, a highly regarded columnist for a major newspaper is quoted as having said: "A person must try to worry about things that aren't important so he won't worry about things that are." The suggestion is well taken, especially if it comes to worrying about major changes at home while one's career falls apart.

Whatever your life, you probably have experienced some family "worry spheres." When you permit these legitimate concerns to spill into your job performance, your career often suffers.

How does one keep family problems out of the workplace? It may sound confusing and contradictory, but having a problem outside the workplace can often become a career advantage. This happens when the employee learns to escape temporarily the personal dilemma by devoting more effort to his or her job.

When Gregory's marriage fell apart, he felt terrible. To keep things together, he threw himself into work. He said to himself: "If I let my personal life damage my career, I will be a double victim. I refuse to let this happen."

Once Sheri knew her ex-husband had skipped town and left her with two children to raise, she buried herself in her job. It helped her not to dwell on negatives and improved her role as a provider. She told herself: "I'll show everybody I can make it as a single mother."

Mrs. Smith, a corporate executive in her fifties, was being torn apart by her thirty year old son who was constantly in trouble. Rather than drive her friends away by talking about it, she devoted most of her effort to her career. She said: "I cannot control the life of my son, but I can enhance my own through a good career."

THREE COMMON MISUNDERSTANDINGS

Sometimes, without being aware it is taking place, we fall into situations that needlessly turn people against us. Have any of the following happened to you?

1 FAILURE TO GIVE OTHERS A SECOND CHANCE.
It is true that we do not always get a second chance to make a good first impression with others. But we may lose more than we suspect when we refuse to give people a second chance to build a relationship with *us*.

> When Brenda first met Cynthia (both were new managers hired from the outside) she decided not to pursue a relationship with Cynthia when Cynthia mishandled their first few moments together. As a result, Brenda did not give Cynthia a second chance. A year later, when Cynthia became Brenda's boss Brenda realized she had needlessly damaged her career.

2 EXPECTING MANAGEMENT TO PROVIDE MOTIVATION.
When we hold management responsible for providing us with productivity incentives to keep us positive, we usually miss the boat and wonder why things didn't turn out well.

> Within two months after employment Sal decided no one cared about his productivity and he turned negative. His productivity dropped to below where it was when he first started. This led to a counseling session with his supervisor. She stated that the company was providing the best possible working environment and Sal was responsible for his attitude and motivation. Sal took exception to her advice and resigned. When his next job (which took him six months to get) provided a working environment less attractive than the one he left, Sal began to understand that attitude and motivation are ''do-it-yourself'' projects in all environments.

3 RELEASING FRUSTRATIONS
Psychologists tell us it is healthy to blow off a little steam now and then. But when this is done in front of co-workers, damage to relationships can occur.

> Stella became so frustrated with her boss two weeks ago that she stormed out of the office and didn't return until the next day. Although Stella and her boss patched things up, there was little she could do to restore relationships with co-workers who witnessed the incident. Stella had to learn the hard way to release her frustrations in a harmless manner away from work.

I—SUMMARY

☐ ...oyees, including managers, underestimate the importance of ...ng strong human relations. These individuals do not bother to learn good human relations skills and in the process slow their career progress.

☐ Human relations competencies (of which there are many) are perhaps more important to career success than are technical skills.

☐ A positive attitude plays a key role in the success of human relationships.

☐ Good communciation is the life-blood of all strong relationships.

☐ One way to avoid harmful damaging of a relationship is to not be overly sensitive to minor personality differences at the other end of the relationship line.

☐ Utilization of the Mutual Reward Theory will help build, maintain, and/or repair important relationships.

☐ Most employees who are consistently late to work or frequently absent, damage relationships because others must do assigned work for them.

☐ There is a direct correlation between how team members relate to each other and the ensuing productivity.

☐ Maintaining good human relations during career plateau periods is critical to one's ability to progress at work.

☐ Employees who are ''human relations smart'' make an honest attempt to repair damaged relationships by initiating positive action as soon as possible. They do this even when the other party is primarily at fault.

PART II

REPAIRING HUMAN RELATIONSHIPS

Some Relationships Will Be Easier To Repair Than Others

THE WILLINGNESS FACTOR

Like abandoned old cars, many relationships are left on the side of the road unrepaired. Even when the restoration of a relationship is important to an individual's career, often no real effort is made to "fix things." Many individuals choose to walk away from a promising situation rather than restore a damaged relationship. It is sometimes difficult to understand why.

One reason may be because one party is reluctant or *unwilling* to discuss the matter. The only way to correct this is to initiate a conversation with that person. A comfortable way this can be accomplished is to make an open statement such as: "Our relationship is important to me, and I am anxious to know what it will take to repair and maintain it." Of course, every person must design an approach that fits his or her "comfort zone." To assist you in initiating such a discussion one of the following tips may help.

- Find something amusing to share.
- Become a better listener.
- Be willing to give a little more than you receive.
- Let the other party "save face."

The restoration of any relationship rests on a willingness of both parties to try. With honest willingness on your part, you may discover the same attitude at the other end of the line. Simply making the effort to talk about "fixing things" could turn you into a human relations winner.

What have you really got to lose?

RELATIONSHIP REPAIR ASSESSMENT EXERCISE

Most relationship conflicts are repairable. A few are not. Many times individuals are so ambivalent about trying to restore a relationship that they back away without making an effort. The purpose of the following exercise is to prevent you from doing this. If you come up with "yes" answers to many of the questions below you should go all out to repair any damage no matter who caused it in the first place. Results will be best if you think about a "real" relationship conflict you are facing. Please answer all questions.

YOUR RELATIONSHIP CONFLICT—ASK YOURSELF: YES NO

1. Is the relationship in question important to your future. ☐ ☐

2. Has the relationship been rewarding in the past? ☐ ☐

3. Do you have a willingness to openly communicate about the conflict? ☐ ☐

4. Are you willing to sit down and discuss possible solutions with the other party? ☐ ☐

5. Would you consider initiating a meeting with the other person regardless of how the conflict started? ☐ ☐

6. If restoration attempts fail, will you consider yourself the primary victim? ☐ ☐

7. If restoration fails, will others also become victims? ☐ ☐

8. Do you honestly want the party at the other end of the relationship line to feel like the relationship has been resolved? ☐ ☐

9. Can you ignore irritating personality traits in order to repair the relationship? ☐ ☐

10. Can you forgive and forget? ☐ ☐

NUMBER OF YES ANSWERS ☐

If you gave 8 or more YES answers, the restoration possibilities are excellent. You should not hesitate to arrange a meeting. Four or more YES answers indicate the restoration possibilities are very good. Three or fewer YES answers is a signal that restoration attempts may be a long shot.

OPEN COMMUNICATION

If good communcation is the life blood of any healthy relationship, then a transfusion of free, open communication should be the first order of business in any relationship repair. It is important to select the right time (when you think the other party will be receptive), the right place (private and free from interruptions), and the discussion should open in a quiet, non-threatening manner.

Once the time and place are ''right'' and both parties are comfortable, you should state in your own way that you would like to discuss a ''win-win'' system that will restore the relationship and keep it healthy. You should invite the other party to describe what it will take to adjust the system so that both parties will benefit in the future.

> It took Jeanne three days to gather up her nerve and select the right time to open a discussion with Harry over their recent "falling out." Although she was awkward in getting the conversation going and introducing her interpretation of a "win-win" theory, Harry picked up on the idea and within twenty minutes they had constructed a new reward system that formed the basis of a new and better working relationship.

MRT, (or ''win-win'') is only one approach that can be used to restore a relationship. You may wish to employ another that fits better into your ''comfort zone.''

RESOLVING CONFLICT

RESOLVING CONFLICTS

Robert B. Maddux in his book *Team Building: An Exercise in Leadership** points out there are many styles in conflict resolution as illustrated below.

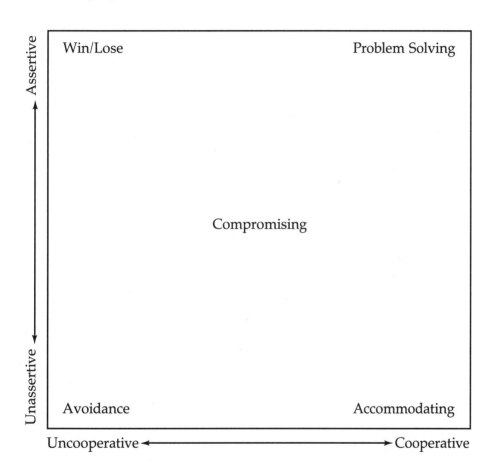

Interpreting the above graphic indicates that if one is unassertive and uncooperative the style is *avoidance*; if one is unassertive and cooperative he or she is *accommodating*; if one is assertive and uncooperative she or he is playing a *win/lose* game. Obviously, when one is assertive, cooperative, and compromising, conflict resolution is more apt to take place. Even when differences exist, the key is willingness to compromise.

**Team Building: An Exercise in Leadership* may be ordered using the information in the back of this book.

COMPROMISE OR BE VICTIMIZED?

In most one-on-one human situations, some compromise is necessary if the relationship is to be maintained. Often a little ''give'' from one end will do the trick. More often, both parties must ''soften'' their position from time to time.

Why is compromise often so difficult?

One reason may be because many people establish such rigid and defiant positions to begin with that any compromise could be interpreted as ''weakness'' or ''failure.''

> Grenville took such a firm stand with his boss about not accepting a temporary assignment that he could not make himself compromise. Later, he discovered his stand had caused a serious conflict and he had second thoughts about compromising but it was too late.

From an MRT perspective, a ''compromise'' often simply means shifting some benefits or rewards. Rather than ''giving in'' and perhaps losing face, one party may agree to provide a different reward than anticipated in exchange for a substitute that is better than the one currently being received.

> Under a corporate flexitime schedule, Jill needed to delay arriving at work until 9:00 a.m. instead of an 8:00 a.m. starting time so she could drop her daughter off at school. The only one in the department Jill could find to cover for her was Sandy who was single. When Jill approached Sandy, she was testy about making the change until the boss explained that the earlier starting time would give Sandy an opportunity to operate a new machine that would improve her skills. Sandy quickly compromised and accepted the new work schedule.

When there is a ''stand off'' between two people, a substitution of rewards can sometimes create two winners.

SOMETIMES COMPROMISE IS NECESSARY

RESTORING A DAMAGED RELATIONSHIP WITH A SUPERIOR

Your most important working relationship is with your immediate superior. If something damages this sensitive relationship, (no matter who is at fault), immediate repair work is recommended.

How do you go about this?

The first thing to remember is that you do not want to allow a small injury to become a major one. Think through the issue. Just how are you being affected? Test your perceptions with a friend who is qualified to weigh the problem from a more objective point of view.

Second, select the right time to approach your superior. She or he may be too busy (or upset about other problems) on a given day to talk with you. If so, wait it out. Pick a time (and place) when you can talk freely and your boss has time to talk things out.

Remember that not all superiors are comfortable with their roles. In fact most people are not well trained in conflict resolution. They may genuinely want to be sensitive and fair, but lack of experience, technique, or pressures interfere. Do not expect perfection. Be satisfied with the best repair job that can be put together under the circumstances.

SOME BOSSES WILL BE EASIER
TO WORK WITH THAN OTHERS

JUST DO IT!

RESTORING A DAMANGED RELATIONSHIP WITH A SUPERIOR (Continued)

Keep in mind that you should be more interested in repairing the relationship than creating any behavioral changes on the part of your boss which would accommodate your needs. Your manager is entitled to his or her personality, just as you are entitled to yours.

When in the process of rebuilding a relationship with a superior, the following suggestions can assist you in reaching a full restoration. You should:

- Keep your personal productivity high.
- Maintain positive relationships with your co-workers.
- Communicate through your attitude that you value your work.
- Refuse to ''bad mouth'' your supervisor in front of others.

If you permit a superior to intimidate you, a healthy, two-way relationship will be impossible. Chances are in your favor this is not the case because most superiors know they are measured by the performance of their staff.

<table>
<tr><td>CASE #
3</td><td></td></tr>
</table>

CASE # 3

RELATIONSHIP REVERSAL

Three years ago Mr. J was promoted to the position of office manager in a large financial institution. He quickly discovered his new boss had trouble communicating. She was abrupt and didn't seem at all interested in Mr. J's career.

When discussing his boss's communication problems with his wife, she suggested he schedule a discussion with her to discuss how they could best work together. At the first opportunity, Mr. J asked his boss what he could contribute in his new role. The next day, Mr. J summarized his boss's expectations and delivered a list of work-oriented goals based on her comments. Mr. J asked his boss to critique them. Slowly, by delivering some of the output his boss wanted, the items he wanted (such as more open communication) began to be forthcoming. Eventually a solid relationship emerged, and Mr. J was recently named as a replacement to his boss who was also promoted.

In using the MRT approach, did Mr. J forestall a conflict that might have turned him into a victim? To compare your answer to that of the author, turn to page 68.

DEALING WITH SHARKS

Near every school of salt water fish, you find a few sharks, (or other predators). In every work environment the likelihood of finding a similar over-aggressive (sometimes unscrupulous) co-worker is present. These individuals can be so devious and insensitive that it does not bother them to make you (or others) victims.

How do you deal with these "sharks?"

First and foremost, it is vital to understand that predators usually thrive on passive souls. At first, they may appear hostile to those who stand up to them (harsh reactions are typical), but often they silently respect (or fear) competitors. So the first thing to do is to let a "shark" know he or she will have trouble making a victim out of you. When forced, you too can be tough.

Victoria was using every technique in the book to undercut Patsy in order to get the new job co-workers knew Patsy had earned. Yesterday Patsy invited Victoria for coffee and said: "Victoria, my career is as important to me as yours is to you. I don't mind competition, but I want you to know that I do not intend to become a victim. Don't let my name Patsy fool you. I'm not. Fair?"

In building relationships with sharks, it is always a good idea to keep the following in mind:

- Do not expect your superior or co-workers to protect you.

- Often, after a confrontation, an improved relationship can be built.

- Those who find they have an emotional reaction after standing up to others should seek the support of others away from work to help diminish the side effects.

CASE #4

CASE
4

BILL AND PHIL

Both Bill and Phil started their careers in a large organization at the same time. It soon became obvious, however, that their philosophy toward work was radically different.

A quiet, introspective person, Bill does his best to maintain soft, comfortable relationships in all directions. Phil is more competitive. He enjoys confrontations. Phil has learned that if he can upset another person emotionally he often comes out ahead. He has the ability to handle heated situations better than others. Phil does not feel guilty when it comes to using this technique. So far Phil's strategy seems to be working. Although younger than Bill, he occupies a more responsible position.

How would you advise people like Bill to deal with those like Phil? To compare your answer with those of the author turn to page 69.

"I'D LIKE YOU TO SEE THINGS MY WAY, BILL!"

PART II SUMMARY

☐ The first step in repairing a relationship is a willingness to communicate.

☐ The MRT approach to resolving a conflict may be your best bet.

☐ Conflict resolution usually includes some degree of compromise from each party.

☐ It often takes all of the tools in one's repair kit to restore a relationship with a supervisor.

☐ ''Sharks'' are less likely to attack co-workers who stand up to them.

PART III

THE SELF-VICTIMIZATION PROCESS

Beware Of Pitfalls

"Skepticism is a hedge against vulnerability."
Charles Thomas Samuels

MID—COURSE REVIEW

The premise of this book is that those who develop and practice sound human relations competencies will enjoy greater career success. A corollary is that those who build healthy working relationships are less apt to be victimized by others.

This does not mean, however, that those who become human relations smart and learn how to repair relationships effectively will not on occasion victimize themselves. They will! That is why what follows (Part III) should be viewed as a significant aspect of human relations education.

Only by knowing how and why people unnecessarily victimize themselves (and learning how to prevent it from happening to you) can you achieve the full benefits of **WINNING AT HUMAN RELATIONS.**

UNDERSTANDING THE SELF-VICTIMIZING PROCESS

Many times a conflict will emerge within a relationship and both parties become increasingly involved in an emotional/psychological process that accelerates into higher and more damaging stages. Three such stages are:

Stage 1: Surface damage with low "hurt" involvement within individuals. Restoration possibilities are excellent if action is taken immediately by either party. No harm, no foul.

Stage 2: Deeper damage to relationship. Emotional "hurt" may be more serious within one individual than the other. Restoration becomes more difficult. One individual is often on the way to becoming a victim.

Stage 3: Emotional/psychological conflict severe. Both parties are often victimized. Restoration often depends upon the willingness of both parties to communicate openly. Professional counseling may be needed.

The process will vary depending on the individuals and the nature of the conflict. But the point is, that once started it is often a continuous development until one or both parties become "losers." Even if one party removes his or herself from the situation (i.e. "bails out"), self-victimization can continue.

The sooner any damage, no matter how slight, is repaired the better. Just as both individuals can lose, if proper timely action is taken, both can also win.

THE PRICE IS HIGH

When people are unfortunate enough to be the victim of either an unintentional accident or a deliberate crime, they often pay a terrible price. The consequences can be similarly serious if and when we become a human relations victim. In extreme cases, it can affect our lifelong career progress. Consider the following.

- Statistically only a small percent of people become victims of a serious crime. Everyone eventually becomes a victim of a damaged relationship.

- Financial loss due to robbery, fraud, or physical injury can be high. So can the loss of a career opportunity.

- The emotional and psychological damage of being a human relations victim can sometimes be as traumatic as being a victim of a crime.

Human conflicts can tear people apart emotionally. Often they are affected so much their productivity drops. It is not unusual for people to turn negative and lose sight of their goals. Becoming a psychological victim of a damaged relationship can cause moodiness, a loss of confidence, resentment, indignation, mental distress and in extreme cases, violence.

More employees resign because of a relationship conflict than for any other reason. Has it ever happened to you?

STAYING ON HOLD FOR TWENTY MINUTES
IS A FORM OF SELF-VICTIMIZATION

IMPACT ON CAREER PROGRESS

In almost any human relations conflict you either wind up as a winner (by resolving the situation) or a loser by becoming a victim.

Last week Hazel and Gena got into an argument over a minor matter involving work schedules. Emotions ran high. Gena adjusted within the hour, but Hazel took the incident personally and sulked around the office for the rest of the week. Her productivity dropped and her supervisor noticed an uncustomary negative attitude toward co-workers and customers alike. In a human relations sense, Gena outsmarted Hazel by refusing to victimize herself over a trivial matter.

Once a conflict occurs, your goal should be to repair the relationship as soon as possible without hurting yourself or the other party. It is difficult to make career progress if you leave a trail of damaged relationships behind you. Also, a primary concern should be the psychological damage you are capable of doing to yourself. Human relations mistakes (no one is immune) are damaging enough when we quickly resolve the issues. But when we internalize the conflict and victimize ourselves, the damage is compounded.

Victimization can occur in many ways. Sometimes it is being overly sensitive to small matters (minor rebuffs, unintentional slights, etc.). At other times, major problems such as deep-seated personality conflicts like prejudice can cause severe damage to our self-esteem. There are also times when we permit conflicts away from work to spill over into the workplace and damage our careers. All of us, on occasion deal with fragile, awkward, human relations situations. When we can handle these without victimizing ourselves, we benefit. By learning how to deal with diverse personalities, we demonstrate we are ''human relations smart'' and become true winners.

AWARENESS EXERCISE

This exercise is designed to help you become more aware of how everyday situations can needlessly make you a victim. First, study each situation. Next, prioritize the list by placing #1 in the square opposite the statement that is most likely to turn you into a victim, a #2 opposite the next most likely situation and so on. Please add your own "touchy" points at the bottom.

☐ Embarrassing yourself by becoming publicly upset over slow service.

☐ Replaying a minor human relations mistake in your mind until you lose sleep over it.

☐ Refusing to apologize over a small human relations error.

☐ Holding a grudge over a simple mistake made by another person.

☐ Refusing to let another person apologize for being insensitive to you.

☐ Becoming furious over a bill that seems too large, or was sent in error.

☐ Over-committing to one co-worker at the expense of damaging good relationships with other team members.

☐ Getting frustrated with a computer or other device because it will not work properly for you.

☐ Becoming frustrated trying to fight the bureaucracy at "city hall."

☐ Allowing someone who doesn't follow-through to your expectations to increase your blood pressure.

OTHER SITUATIONS:

☐ _____

☐ _____

☐ _____

THREE WAYS PEOPLE VICTIMIZE THEMSELVES

1. WHEN THEY REFUSE TO CORRECT MISTAKES QUICKLY.

> José knew he had offended Ralph when he neglected to include him in a decision-making meeting. Quickly, he apologized, stated how he valued their relationship and invited him to lunch. Before lunch had ended the relationship had been fully restored.

2. WHEN THEY PERMIT A 'NO FAULT' SITUATION TO GO UNANSWERED.

> It became obvious to everyone but Pat that the misunderstanding was nobody's fault and a classic, almost laughable case of miscommunication. Even so, Robert, the only one who could be deeply hurt by the situation, played it safe and took Pat out to dinner to discuss what happened and make certain their relationship was back on sound footing. When asked by a co-worker why he took the initiative Robert replied: ''Nobody was at fault, but I didn't want to gamble and wind up becoming a victim because Pat didn't see the big picture.''

3. WHEN THEY PERMIT THE EMOTIONALISM OF A RELATIONSHIP CONFLICT TO CHEW THEM UP INSIDE.

> When John and Mr. Andrew got into a conflict, John internalized the situation to the point he couldn't sleep at night. Soon his productivity dropped. Mr. Andrew, with more experience and objectivity, was able to pass off the emotional side more easily. Result? John remained so bothered by the incident that he resigned-even though he liked his job. John became the primary victim.

WHO WILL BECOME THE VICTIM?
(An Exercise)

The temptation to blame others for normal human problems is natural. Still, even when others are at fault, we can become a victim. Listed below are some typical workplace problems. As you read them, please ask yourself the question: "Who will become the ultimate victim?"

You blow off steam about an irritating habit of your boss and the word gets back to him.

A co-worker is a "know-it-all" and you permit it to get under your skin?

You and your boss have a fundamental communications misunderstanding over deadlines.

A careless co-worker forgets to tell you about an important telephone call from a customer and you lose the account.

Your boss, under pressure, comes down on you heavily in front of the office staff but apologizes in private the next day.

To your bitter disappointment your request to attend an out-of-state meeting is turned down.

You discover your boss accepted an idea you discussed with a co-worker a few weeks ago and gave that person credit.

You discover a fellow employee has "blown the whistle" on you for unintentionally violating a safety rule.

How you react in the above situations could turn you into a victim. It is a difficult lesson to learn, but as far as being a victim is concerned it often doesn't matter who is at fault. When faced with similar situations in the future, why not send yourself a warning signal by asking the following question?

> ### AM I BECOMING A VICTIM?

HIGH-RISK WORKING RELATIONSHIPS

Generally speaking, the more meaningful a relationship is, the more risk is involved for becoming deeply hurt when damage occurs. This is *The High Involvement High Vulnerability Principle.* It states that the more involved and intense a relationship becomes, the more vulnerable you are to being ''hurt'' if a conflict arises. Three critical factors are involved in all working relationships.

Frequency of Contact: If you have a conflict with a person you work with on a daily basis, you are more apt to be a victim than if the conflict is with a more distant co-worker. Daily contact can intensify a conflict even though the opportunity for communication (and resolve) is present.

Nature of Relationship: Your relationship with your superior is far more complex than with that of most co-workers. Such factors as authority, performance appraisals, discipline, are involved. The maintenance of a relationship with a superior often requires more attention, care, and perception.

Personal Involvement: The better you know a co-worker on a personal basis, the more sensitive it can become if a conflict surfaces. This is the reason many experienced workers choose to keep their personal and working relationships separate.

Some working relationships require more maintenance than do others. In most cases, these ''high involvement individuals'' are the people who will come to your support when needed. But they can also damage you the most in conflict situations.

Have you ever personally experienced The High Involvement High Vulnerability Principle?

YOUR CO-WORKERS MAY EXPRESS SYMPATHY TOWARD A RELATIONSHIP CONFLICT YOU ARE EXPERIENCING WHILE AT THE SAME TIME SITTING BACK AND WONDERING WHY YOU ARE SO INTENT ON VICTIMIZING YOURSELF.

A VICTIM-PRONE RELATIONSHIP

Outside of a marriage, no arrangement places more demands on The Mutual Reward Theory than a 50/50 business partnership. This is true because the legal structure of a partnership is designed to establish an equal reward system that is virtually impossible to maintain. Each partner is supposed to contribute equal energy, talent, hours, and capital to the success of the business. When one partner perceives that the other is not contributing as much as the other, a conflict can surface.

Bess and Carol Ann decided to open a day-care center on a 50/50 partnership basis. They spent hundreds of hours researching and planning the operation. But neither took time for a close look at the *kind* of relationship they could develop and maintain. Were they compatible? Did they understand the division of duties? Could they make it work? After both families contributed their savings (and took out second mortgages), the operation was launched with great success. The profit the first year was greater than either Bess or Carol Ann had hoped to achieve. Even so, the business eventually failed. Neither Bess or Carol Ann could maintain an ongoing acceptable working relationship because neither could agree on the level of contribution the other was making to the business.

Few relationships demand as much as a business partnership, but *all* relationships have a stress factor. When the stress falls more heavily on one person than the other, that individual is vulnerable to becoming a primary victim. Although Bess and Carol Ann became financial victims because their business failed, the more serious damage was emotional because it broke up a twenty year friendship.

CASE #5

<table>
<tr><td>CASE #
5</td><td># THE VULNERABLE PROFESSOR</td></tr>
</table>

THE VULNERABLE PROFESSOR

Dr. Franklin was highly regarded by his colleagues at Apex University. He was treated with sensitivity and given every consideration. When he decided to expand his department, Professor Franklin was given immediate authority to recruit and hire an assistant.

After several interviews, he selected a much younger, but highly qualified individual. For the first year, they appeared to have a solid working relationship. Then philosophical differences surfaced and their students began to divide themselves into the camp of either Dr. Franklin or his assistant. Soon, the professors started to avoid each other. Then they stopped communicating completely. Without communication the conflict intensified. Four years later, Dr. Franklin took early retirement to avoid further emotional distress. To those aware of what was going on, it became obvious that Dr. Franklin had become the primary victim.

What might Dr. Franklin have done in the early stages to avoid the conflict? What corrective steps might he have taken to restore the relationship? Is it a fair statement to say that Dr. Franklin victimized himself?

Compare your answers with those of the author on page 69.

IT'S FINE TO STAND
ON A PRINCIPLE THAT
IS IMPORTANT TO
YOU . . . PROVIDING
YOU DON'T GET SO
EMOTIONALLY
ENTANGLED THAT
YOU VICTIMIZE
YOURSELF.

KNOWING YOUR VULNERABILITY

Sometimes it is important to defend a principle even though it is controversial and will create a conflict. An important consideration in taking such a position, is whether or not you will victimize yourself.

For many reasons (sibling rivalry, family training, cultural background, etc.) some people more easily throw off the emotions that accompany conflict. Others will internalize and allow the conflict to seriously disrupt their lives.

> Marci and Janice would go into a management meeting with the same amount of enthusiasm. If the meeting was non-controversial, they would leave the same way they entered. However, if emotions ran high, Marci could throw it off before leaving work while Janice would lose sleep and not overcome the effect of the conflict for several days.

Those who are unable to keep relationship conflicts from ''getting under their skin'' are more vulnerable to self-victimization than those blessed with the ability to step back. As a result, they need to learn to play their cards differently. This may mean taking a closer look at the principle to see if it is worth defending or perhaps better advance preparation in order to remain more objective or in some cases finding an acceptable compromise or substitute.

If you wish to become a martyr, make sure the issue warrants it. Only when there is a severe violation of your values should you leave a job. If it is a difference of opinion, you must remember that you could be wrong. Study the opposing view with an open mind to make certain of your position. If you are wrong, it can be a positive learning experience instead of a major career change.

Becoming a martyr in most business environments is a good way to permanently screw-up your career progress.

WHY ARE PEOPLE BLIND TO SELF-VICTIMIZATION?

When individuals discover they are involved in a relationship conflict, few have the insight or experience to back away and get the "bigger picture" before making an effort at restoration. Once an individual learns how to do this, he or she might approach the same situation differently, with far better results.

> Joe became so distressed over the relationship with his new boss that he almost resigned on the spot. Controlling his emotions, he and a friend took time to evaluate the conflict. When Joe and his friend assessed the situation from all angles (Joe's seniority, experience, corporate friends, image, etc.), it became clear that Joe would become a needless victim if his boss won. It was hard on Joe's ego but he decided to compromise and work to rebuild the relationship. Today Joe is a senior manager in the organization and his former superior is no longer around.

There are three basic factors that make it difficult to see the forest (your career) from the trees (your current emotional stress.) They are:

1. FALLING FOR THE "EYE FOR AN EYE" SYNDROME.

When an employee is under stress from a relationship conflict, it is natural to blame the other person.

> When the sales manager gave a choice sales territory to Bernadette, Frank exploded. He laid the blame at the door of the sales manager. His hostility cost him being considered for the position of assistant sales manager (a better opportunity than staying in the field) which was to be reviewed in a few weeks. As a result of the turmoil, Frank resigned to "save face." Looking back, Frank knows he victimized himself and blew a good career possibility with a quality company.

WHY ARE PEOPLE BLIND TO SELF-VICTIMIZATION (Continued)

2. ACCEPTING ADVICE FROM THE WRONG SOURCES.

When a relationship conflict surfaces, it is possible to gain a better perspective by talking things over with another person. *But not always.* The wrong person can pour fuel on the fire and the situation can intensify, pushing both parties farther away from a solution.

> Millie was so upset emotionally when the promotion was given to Jeremy that she needed to talk to someone. She chose Geraldine and Victoria. Neither of them knew all of the facts, and they persuaded Millie to file a sex discrimination suit. The preliminary investigation of the suit showed that Jeremy was more highly qualified and that management had made a sound decision. By the time Millie backed away from the investigation, her relationship with Geraldine and Victoria had ended. Millie realized she had unnecessarily victimized herself because of poor advice from two co-workers.

Talking the issue out with an objective observer (Geraldine and Victoria were not objective) can dissipate some of the pain and better classify the issue. A few possibilities might be (1) Someone in the Human Resource Department. (2) A mentor. (3) A more senior person with whom you can share a confidence.

3. LETTING YOUR EGO STAND IN THE WAY.

When it comes to relationships, everyone makes mistakes. Frequently, those with experience, and positive self-esteem make simple misjudgements that one might expect from an inexperienced employee. When this happens, the ''ego'' of the ''pro'' can get in the way of a victimless solution.

> Mr. Judson found it humiliating when the quarterly report showed that Ms. Kay, a new manager of a branch operation similar to his, had beaten his previous quarterly sales record. The next time he and Ms. Kay met, Mr. J was demeaning in his comments and initiated a conflict that became common knowledge around the firm. In the months that followed Mr. J tried so hard to beat Ms. Kay, that he neglected other aspects of his responsibilities. Eventually the company president was forced to counsel Mr. Judson. Result? Ms. Kay received a promotion that Mr. J could have received if his ego had not gotten in the way.

In the area of human relationships, it is very possible to ''win a battle and lose the war''. An individual can become so involved in the psychology of the conflict that he or she fails to recognize that self-destruction is happening.

| CASE #
6 | DISPOSABLE RELATIONSHIPS |

In all of her thirty-two years Denise had never felt more victimized. Her career path had been placed on hold because of corporate ''downsizing'', a trusted co-worker had done a number on her, and she was extremely upset by the conflict in her divorce proceedings that had been going on for several weeks.

Talking to her sister, Dorothy, she commented: ''Sis, I've decided never to enter a serious relationship again. That way, when they don't work out I can toss them. Meaningful relationships in all aspects of my life have a way of kicking me in the face.''

Dorothy replied: ''I disagree. We all need meaningful relationships, both at work and in our personal lives. It's quality, not quantity. I believe you should stay in the mainstream and enjoy people. But you also must learn to grow up and find a way to develop and maintain *good* relationships. It's not the number of flowers in your garden, it's the beauty of those you nurture. Your problem is that every time a relationship goes bad, you feel sorry for yourself and become more of a loner. If you don't learn to build and protect rewarding relationships, you will continue to victimize yourself. You are going to turn into a recluse.''

What flaws, if any, do you find in Dorothy's argument? Is she guilty of being simplistic in her approach? Compare your thoughts with those of the author on page 69.

PART III SUMMARY

☐ Only a few of us become victims of serious crimes, but eventually each of us become a human relations victim.

☐ The victimization process tends to accelerate unless immediate steps are taken to resolve the conflict.

☐ You can become a primary victim even if you are not at fault.

☐ Self-victimization occurs when one cannot handle the emotional strain that goes with a relationship conflict.

☐ Most people are so involved in the emotionalism of a conflict that they are not aware they are victimizing themselves.

PART IV

PREPARING A WINNING STRATEGY

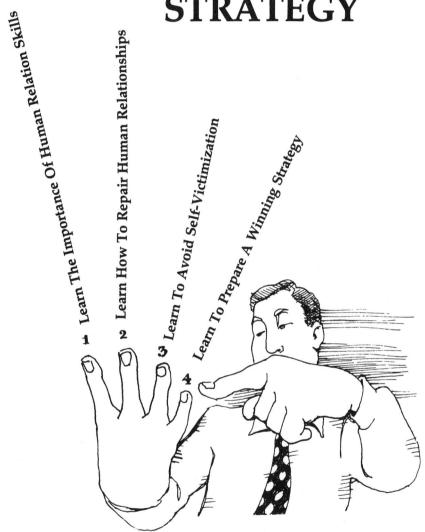

1 **Learn The Importance Of Human Relation Skills**

2 **Learn How To Repair Human Relationships**

3 **Learn To Avoid Self-Victimization**

4 **Learn To Prepare A Winning Strategy**

''Our major obligation is not to mistake slogans for solutions.''
Edward R. Murrow

PUTTING IT ALL TOGETHER

(A QUICK REVIEW AND CHALLENGE)

> ### THE REVIEW

PART I   Demonstrated that by following certain principles, you could build and maintain better relationships with superiors and co-workers.

PART II   Gave you a tested approach to use in the restoration of damaged relationships.

PART III   Explained the self-victimization process to teach you how to do a better job of protecting yourself in future human conflicts.

> ### THE CHALLENGE

PART IV will provide you with an opportunity to put what you have learned into a master strategy. This part presents practical techniques that will help you effectively build and maintain quality relationships. By making progress in all directions you can enhance your career progress and earn the compliment of being called "human relations smart."

THE CHALLENGE!

Ten techniques or tips (one per page) follow. Based upon your experience, insight, and personal style, you are invited to challenge each. To encourage this, please signify at the end of each technique, whether you agree, disagree, or are uncertain by placing a check in the appropriate box. Then review your commitments and work to incorporate those with which you agree into your human relations strategy for the future.

TECHNIQUE #1

CREATE AND MAINTAIN A VARIETY OF RELATIONSHIPS

In any job, there are many relationships to create and maintain. In addition to superiors and co-workers, there are usually clients and key people in other departments that are important to your career progress. A secretary, guard, or maintenance person should not be ignored.

Co-workers, however, deserve special attention for the following reasons.

1. When you help fellow-workers produce more, you enhance your reputation.

> Although Jake's personal productivity was average, management recognized that he was always helping team members with technical problems and contributed to their higher productivity.

2. When you keep a good attendance record and show up on time each day you make things easier for your supervisor and co-workers.

> Although Alice was slower than others in serving customers, she was never late and seldom absent. Whenever another department member didn't show, Alice picked up the slack without complaining.

3. When co-workers like you they can influence management to promote you.

> Sylvester, through his positive attitude earned the respect of co-workers as well as superiors. When the role of manager opened up, three co-workers told management they could work well with Sylvester.

Other relationships should not be neglected. But for those who want to impress management that they are human relations smart, an excellent place to demonstrate such skills is with co-workers.

AGREE	DISAGREE	UNCERTAIN
☐	☐	☐

TECHNIQUE #2

SEE RELATIONSHIPS—NOT PERSONALITIES

You will take a major step in improving relationships and avoiding conflicts when you learn to concentrate on the relationship, *not* the personality at the end of the relationship line. Easy to say, sometimes hard to accomplish!

> Mrs. M. had high personal standards of grooming and social grace. She could find little ''right'' with her co-worker Mr. K. Without sensing the negative implications, she often tore him down in public by commenting on his lack of polish. When her superior suggested she look at the contribution Mr. K was making to the department and not at his personal habits of dress or imperfect grammar, her attitude started to change. Although it would not be Mrs. M's choice to mix socially with Mr. K, she recognized that he was a career professional with many unique talents.

To keep working relationships in good order, it is best to observe what people do rather than what they seem to be on the surface. Work habits are important on the job not minor personality quirks. Do your colleagues do their best to carry a full load? Do they cooperate and work well with others? Are they willing to learn? Do they have special talents that contribute to team productivity?

Professional employees should deal with working relationships and attempt to stay away from a critical analysis of personalities. Those who deal in what can be called ''personality assassinations'' create human conflicts and can easily wind up as victims.

AGREE	DISAGREE	UNCERTAIN
☐	☐	☐

TECHNIQUE #3

PRACTICE THE MUTUAL REWARD THEORY

When it comes to a one-on-one session with an individual with whom there is a conflict, a direct approach is not always the best. For many people a confrontation may be too stressful and uncomfortable. Answer? A better plan may be to initiate a discussion that develops a MUTUAL REWARD approach.

The Mutual Reward Theory states that for a human relationship to remain healthy over an extended period of time the benefits should be somewhat equal between both parties. What is important is that each participant views what they receive from the relationship as ''satisfactory'' to them. Both individuals should feel they come out ahead. The idea is to introduce the mutual reward concept with the other party.

> Jake, sensing that his on-the-job relationship with Freda was deteriorating, set up a meeting in her office and said: ''Freda, up until now we have worked well together. But I get the feeling we are beginning to work against each other instead of pulling together. I would like to get your ideas on how we can keep our mutual support system working.''

Using the mutual reward idea is a good idea because it takes an oblique rather than a confrontational approach. Not only is it easier to use, but with open communication a more satisfactory reward mix usually develops. In almost all relationship conflicts, reconciliation depends upon the creation of a more satisfactory reward system. This is the true meaning of ''give and take'' or ''compromise'' in conflict resolution.

AGREE	DISAGREE	UNCERTAIN
☐	☐	☐

TECHNIQUE #4

LET SMALL IRRITATIONS PASS

> Years ago my wife and I were waiting for a valet to bring our car to the front of a restaurant where we had enjoyed a delightful dinner. When the car arrived I noticed a large dent in the rear fender and immediately blew my top. After embarrassing both my wife and myself, we discovered the valet had brought another customer's car that was identical to ours. Our car was fine. I didn't sleep well that night, but it was my fault. I had blown my stack before properly assessing the situation. I had victimized myself.

How many times have you seen anyone come away the winner when they made a fuss over slow service in a restaurant or complained to a postal employee? Did they really win when they told somebody off on the telephone or became angry in a traffic jam? Or, worst of all, explode in the work environment?

You might feel it is good to "blow off some steam," but in most cases similar to the above, a "short fuse" person either hurts his or her image, or winds up embarrassed and feeling foolish. Even worse, if you "blew up" over a minor irritation that was nobody's fault and then recognized it later as being "dumb," it could ruin the rest of your day. The truth is (even though your complaint may have been justifiable) *you* become the victim, not the other party. How can you prevent this from happening?

1. Work on detaching yourself emotionally from the upsetting trivials of life. Tell yourself over and over that "big people handle little irritations with grace."

2. Train yourself to look beyond such incidents. One way to accomplish this is to "walk away" from the irritation counting and reminding yourself that life is too short to worry about minor annoyances. There are more important things to do.

3. Quickly ask yourself "Who will be the victim?"

AGREE	DISAGREE	UNCERTAIN
☐	☐	☐

TECHNIQUE #5

RECOGNIZE WARNING SIGNALS

Most people wear "blinders" when it comes to being victimized by others. Their feelings get hurt; they blame the other party and react without considering the long term. A few individuals follow this pattern over and over.

How can you learn to warn yourself before excessive damage is done to an important relationship?

A first step is to ask the questions:

—Do I have more to lose than the other party?
—Is there still a chance to salvage the relationship?
—Is open communication still a possibility?

The best "early warning" signal is to stay aware of your attitude. Are you starting to react negatively to a person or situation? Are you as positive about your career and the work environment as you were previously?

> On his last formal appraisal, Roger was given a "satisfactory" rating on attitude. His previous rating had been "superior." When Roger asked why, he was told that his enthusiasm and sensitivity to others seemed to have measurably diminshed. Thinking back to a relationship problem that had surfaced in his department, Roger recognized that this was when he had started to turn negative and the change in rating was justified.

Each person is the custodian of his or her attitude. You cannot expect others to tell you when it turns from positive to negative. But if you are honest and in touch with yourself, you know when it happens. When you sense things are out of "tune", evaluate why you feel that way and then turn things around. Your negative attitude may be the best signal that you have to begin rebuilding a relationship before it is too late.

AGREE	DISAGREE	UNCERTAIN
☐	☐	☐

TECHNIQUE #6

CHOOSE ADVISORS CAREFULLY

When relationship conflicts develop there is a critical need to talk things over with others who can be objective. It is also therapeutic to do this. Whom should you select? Upon what basis?

Common sense tells us that it is smart to keep "home based" problems away from work and some work problems away from home. This is especially true when you need to discuss a conflict involving a co-worker or family member. For example, unless you have an outstanding relationship, it is probably best to talk over a serious work conflict with a mature outsider (spouse, friend, or professional counselor). On the other side of the coin, talking freely about a home problem with co-workers may hurt productivity, your image, or possibly damage your relationships at home, especially if word gets back that you have been discussing details of your home life.

Either way, the problem comes in selecting the "right" person to assist you and provide objectivity. Those closest to you may be your logical first choice, but if they are not objective, taking their advice could do more harm than good.

> When Julie had a home problem, her two best friends at work tried to offer advice based on their experiences. Julie welcomed their support, but it only intensified the situation at home and caused confusion and a loss of productivity at work. The delay (eventually Julie found a solution through professional help) damaged her ability to concentrate at work.

So what is the answer?

Discretion!

Choose your "confidants" carefully so your problem will not spill over and disturb other relationships at home or at work. The following suggestions may help.
1. Select an advisor who understands the self-victimization concept and is far enough removed from the problem to be objective.
2. Try not to settle for any "advice" unless both parties in the conflict stand a chance of coming out ahead.
3. Be true to yourself and your judgement.
4. If you receive assistance from a friend consider the help you received as a "reward" and try to return it in the future.

AGREE	DISAGREE	UNCERTAIN
☐	☐	☐

TECHNIQUE #7

HOW TO DISTANCE YOURSELF

When a relationship is important to your career, using good communication to restore any conflict is recommended. But what do you do when you sense a conflict coming from an individual who is only interested in his or her gains and doesn't really care about you?

> In recent weeks Janet has been aware that her co-worker Aaron has been using her to further his career. He disrupts her productivity to learn things he should be learning on his own time. He asks her to "cover" for him while he is playing office politics elsewhere. He is generous in buying drinks after work, but almost all of the conversation is directed to subjects that will enhance his career, not hers. Slowly Janet has decided that their relationship is never going to be mutually rewarding.

Already a victim, how can Janet keep the process from continuing or getting worse?

Withdrawing from any relationship (instead of trying to resolve the conflict) is sometimes a mixed blessing. This is because the relationship is probably satisfying some need or the victimized individual would have pulled away sooner. "Distancing" is a technique in itself. The following tips may help.

1. Go about it slowly even though the co-worker may suspect what is happening.

2. Play it human relations smart by becoming more involved with other co-workers so that other relationships are strengthened.

3. Consider changing lunch and "after work" habits so you will have less contact with the individuals.

Not all co-worker relationship conflicts can be resolved. Doing nothing when you know that the victimization process is operating is wishful thinking. You must learn to distance yourself.

AGREE	DISAGREE	UNCERTAIN
☐	☐	☐

TECHNIQUE #8

WHEN TO COMPROMISE

If you react to any conflict by engaging in an ''eye for an eye'' philosophy, you will quickly victimize yourself by damaging other relationships. Your goal should be either to leave the individual alone or to help that person win (even if he or she created the conflict) because it is the only way *you* can win.

> When Jason heard that Thelma would receive the promotion he expected, his first reaction was to tell his co-workers she was a poor choice. Then, realizing that would damage other relationships because of a ''sour grapes'' approach, Jason changed his mind. Two months later he received a promotion better suited to his talents. Both he and Thelma came out ahead.

Compromising to protect our future without hurting others is human relations smart for many reasons. Here are two:

1. Conflicts that hurt others can ''boomerang'' if management senses productivity has been lowered.

2. Vindictive behavior is never respected by others.

Sometimes compromise is smart for these reasons:

1. It may generate new rewards that you value as much or more than those you lose.

2. When you accept new ideas in the course of a compromise you benefit.

3. Compromise may be the *only* way to restore a relationship.

AGREE	DISAGREE	UNCERTAIN
☐	☐	☐

TECHNIQUE #9

HAVE A "PLAN B" READY

There are two basic ways in which you can become a career victim in today's world.

1. Become a casualty as the result of a human relations problem left unsolved.

2. Become a victim because of an organizational change.

As insurance against either possibility, you should have an alternative career option known as a "Plan B."*

Human relations problems are covered in this book. Organizational changes are not; but they are more frequent today than ever before. Mergers, downsizing, restructuring, and technological advances have increased the intensity of the winds of change. Job security is no longer a given. Outside influences, even if one plays it human relations smart, have the potential to cause problems that make a career change necessary or advisable.

What is a Plan B? It is simply a thoughtful strategy that can be activated on the day you decide on a career change. A professional Plan B is a formalized comprehensive career enhancement program that includes the following action steps. Plan B:

1. Insures you are as efficient as possible in your present job (Plan A).

2. Keeps your job competencies current so you always maintain your "Marketability."

3. Activates a creative networking system to help you locate other, potentially better opportunities.

Because relationship conflicts are always present and the winds of organizational change will continue to intensify, experts are saying today that a career Plan B is a necessity, not an option.

AGREE	DISAGREE	UNCERTAIN
☐	☐	☐

---

*The author has written a comprehensive book *Plan B: Converting Change into Career Opportunity* that can be ordered using the information in the back of this book.

TECHNIQUE #10

YOUR ATTITUDE IS PRICELESS: PROTECT IT!

Most employees are positive when on the job. Their positive, cooperative attitudes contribute to their productivity as well as that of their co-workers. Mature individuals recognize that the moment they turn negative it signals the potential for trouble, including self-victimization.

Readers who are "attitude conscious" are aware of the negative career consequences which reside in a poor attitude. They know it is their personal responsibility to stay as upbeat and productive as possible, no matter what their home or work problems may be. To assist you in staying positive, the following techniques are presented from the book *Attitude: Your Most Priceless Possession* (which may be ordered using the information in the back of this book):

1. USE THE FLIPSIDE TECHNIQUE.
When an irritating problem hits, "flip it over" to see if you can find some humor to soften the blow.

> When Rick discovered someone had creased a fender in his car in the employee parking lot he laughingly announced that he would buy the culprit a drink if his or her insurance protection would help him buy the new car he was already thinking about.

This technique (even if you don't find any humor) may keep you from making a victim out of yourself.

2. PLAY YOUR WINNERS.
The idea is to concentrate on the good things you have going for you so negative issues seem smaller.

> Malinda, having a problem with her supervisor, stayed positive by writing down a positive factor about her job every time she became upset with him. After exhausting all of the positive things she could think of (seven) she decided her job was better than she thought and initiated a meeting with her supervisor to see if things could be improved through better communication.

TECHNIQUE #10

YOUR ATTITUDE IS PRICELESS: PROTECT IT!
(Continued)

3. INSULATE YOURSELF AGAINST MAJOR WORRIES.

When a major problem starts to pull you down, it is psychologically possible to push it to the outer perimeter of your mind so it won't interfere with your productivity.

> Dolores, a popular and respected worker, had to take a week off when her only son was severely injured in an accident. Upon her return, she forced herself to think "work" instead of "hospital" and discovered it really helped her get through her difficult period.

4. SHARE YOUR POSITIVE ATTITUDE WITH OTHERS.

Little can dissipate a negative attitude sooner than doing something special for another person.

> Six months ago when Willie turned negative over a family matter, he brought himself back by doing something special for a different person at work each day. Most of the time it was nothing more than a friendly compliment or an appropriate joke. Now Willie maintains his positive attitude in the same way he recovered it.

5. LOOK BETTER TO YOURSELF.

One way to fight back after you have been victimized (or become negative) is to improve your image.

> When Zelda permitted her attitude to slip during a plateau period that she had not anticipated, she restored it by creating a new image through a new hairstyle, wardrobe, and weight-loss program. When sales improved in her organization, she was immediately promoted.

When it comes to winning at human relations, attitude is your most priceless possession. Anything you can do to keep it consistently positive is a good investment.

AGREE	DISAGREE	UNCERTAIN
☐	☐	☐

PART V

FINAL REVIEW

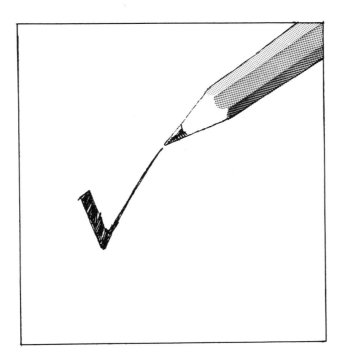

"A little learning is a dangerous thing, but a lot of ignorance is just as bad."
Bob Edwards

SIX QUESTIONS AND ANSWERS

1. *When it comes to human relations, I get the idea that an ounce of prevention is worth a pound of cure. Am I right?*

   Absolutely! Once the self-victimization process starts it is difficult to contain. Thus, the better you become at maintaining relationships the fewer conflicts you will be forced to deal with.

2. *Won't the passage of time cause some working relationship conflicts to disappear without action from either party?*

   Not always. Even when it happens a great deal of distress and loss of productivity can take place until time pushes the conflict into the distance. Open communication at the beginning can often keep this from happening.

3. *What kind of commitment is necessary to win at human relations?*

   A sincere, determined three-part commitment! First, continue to improve your human relations skills. Second, use MRT to restore any broken relationships. Third, recognize that the moment you lose your positive attitude you are victimizing yourself.

4. *Is it possible for one to remain sufficiently positive during a long-term relationship conflict at home so co-workers will not know it is going on?*

   When off-the job problems are severe, it usually impacts job performance. That is one reason employee assistance programs (supported by management) can contribute to productivity.

5. *If people are not used to confronting others who are trying to victimize them, won't taking such a step take an emotional toll?*

   On a temporary basis, yes. But the damage of permitting an intimidating relationship to continue could be far greater. Another advantage is that it probably will not be so difficult (or damaging) the next time it is necessary.

6. *When is enough enough? When should a conflict cause an individual to pack up and leave a job or organization?*

   Once the victimization process between a superior and a worker reaches an advanced stage, it may be time to seek a transfer or look to another firm. A conflict between two co-workers may deserve a softer treatment. All of this assumes that restoration attempts have been made.

TEST YOURSELF

Demonstrate that you are human relations smart by answering the following true and false questions. Correct answers will be found at the end of the exercise.

TRUE FALSE

___ ___ 1. The challenge in this book is to make the most of human relationships without becoming a victim.

___ ___ 2. Most people automatically know how to balance their technical and human relations skills.

___ ___ 3. One can be more objective dealing directly with personalities rather than focusing on the relationship.

___ ___ 4. A mutually rewarding relationship is one where both parties receive somewhat equal but different benefits from each other.

___ ___ 5. A "conflict point" in a relationship can occur when one receives or gives too many "rewards."

___ ___ 6. MRT is a poor approach to use in the restoration of a damaged relationship.

___ ___ 7. Fortunately, the attitude of one employee does not influence the productivity of another.

___ ___ 8. The key to the restoration of any damaged relationship is the willingness of both parties to try.

___ ___ 9. The decision of whether or not to try and repair a damaged relationship depends on who was at fault.

___ ___ 10. People who are human relations smart never victimize themselves.

___ ___ 11. Embarrassing yourself in public does not come under the category of self-victimization.

___ ___ 12. Employees often become victims when they refuse to quickly mend a repairable relationship.

___ ___ 13. The more meaningful a relationship the less apt one is to be victimized by it.

___ ___ 14. Standing on principle does not involve human relationship risks.

___ ___ 15. Business partnerships create few victims.

___ ___ 16. Self-victimization usually occurs when one cannot handle the emotional strain that goes with a relationship conflict.

___ ___ 17. Absenteeism seldom leads one into becoming a career victim.

___ ___ 18. When it comes to a severely damaged relationship within an organization, it is always best to cut your losses by starting over elsewhere.

___ ___ 19. A Plan B can be designed to help you from becoming an organizational victim.

___ ___ 20. Becoming negative may be an early warning that one is being victimized.

ANSWERS: 1.T 2.F 3.F 4.T 5.F 6.F 7.F 8.T 9.F 10.F 11.F 12.T 13.F 14.F 15.F 16.T 17.F 18.F 19.T 20.T

SUGGESTED ANSWERS TO CASES:

SUGGESTED ANSWER TO CASE #1: PAGE 5 JEFF AND HIS BOSS

Jeff has too much invested with his firm not to give the suggestion a serious try. If he resigns or takes early retirement, he could be victimizing himself while his boss gets off free. Once Jeff stops talking about the irritating characteristics of his boss (and discontinues reinforcing them in his mind), he will be better able to concentrate on his responsibilities. This, in turn, will be therapeutic. The relationships between Jeff and his boss may never be fully repaired, but by becoming more objective, Jeff should be able to survive without tearing himself up emotionally until normal personnel changes eliminate the problem. Jeff is already a victim but his actions could cut his losses and restore the upward mobility of his career.

SUGGESTED ANSWER TO CASE #2: PAGE 15 JENNIFER'S IMAGE

Although difficult, through open communication with Vickie at the beginning, Jennifer could have kept their working and social relationships separate. Professional employees are successful at doing this all the time. Inexperience with people was probably the reason it took Jennifer so long to "catch on." In most work environments it is impossible for a high-productivity employee to "carry" a low-productivity employee without damaging her or his image and career progress.

SUGGESTED ANSWER TO CASE #3: PAGE 29 RELATIONSHIP REVERSAL

Sometimes a positive approach to a potential relationship conflict is the only way to keep from being victimized. Mr. J may have saved his career by taking early action. His wife is to be complimented for her insight in recommending the MRT approach.

SUGGESTED ANSWERS TO CASES
(Continued)

SUGGESTED ANSWER TO CASE #4: PAGE 31 PHIL AND BILL

To protect their careers, non-assertive people like Bill need to train themselves to stand up to confrontations without victimizing themselves. The fact that eight-hour seminars are often devoted to the process indicates it is not easy to learn. The following pattern might help Bill get started: (1) Discuss the situation with an objective advisor who is more experienced in confrontations. (2) With the help of this individual, design a strategy that minimizes the possibility of greater conflict. (3) Employ this strategy in a calm manner without rancor or vindictiveness. (4) Whatever happens, try not to take it personally. (5) Return to the original advisor to evaluate results so that improvements continue.

SUGGESTED ANSWER TO CASE #5: PAGE 43 THE VULNERABLE PROFESSOR

Early and open communication between Dr. Franklin and his assistant could have resolved their philosophical differences before they became a conflict point that spilled over to the students. Dr. Franklin should have taken the initiative. The MRT approach could have resolved the conflict. Yes, it is a fair statement to say Dr. Franklin victimized himself. He should have reminded himself that communication is the life blood of any relationship and taken the first step.

SUGGESTED ANSWER TO CASE #6: PAGE 48 DISPOSABLE RELATIONSHIPS

It would appear that Dorothy has become jaded regarding human relations and, as a result, she may have come down too hard on Denise. Many people become human relations victims over and over again without turning into hard, insensitive individuals or recluses. Dorothy sounds like she still carries scars of past victimizations with her.

NOTES

NOTES

NOTES

NOTES

NOTES

NOTES

NOTES

NOW AVAILABLE FROM CRISP PUBLICATIONS

Books • Videos • CD Roms • Computer-Based Training Products

Subject Areas Include:

Management

Human Resources

Communication Skills

Personal Development

Marketing/Sales

Organizational Development

Customer Service/Quality

Computer Skills

Small Business and Entrepreneurship

Adult Literacy and Learning

Life Planning and Retirement

CRISP WORLDWIDE DISTRIBUTION

English language books are distributed worldwide. Major international distributors include:

ASIA/PACIFIC

Australia/New Zealand: In Learning, PO Box 1051 Springwood QLD, Brisbane, Australia 4127
Telephone: 7-3841-1061, Facsimile: 7-3841-1580   ATTN: Messrs. Gordon

Singapore: Graham Brash (Pvt) Ltd. 32, Gul Drive, Singapore 2262
Telephone: 65-861-1336, Facsimile: 65-861-4815   ATTN: Mr. Campbell

CANADA

Reid Publishing, Ltd., Box 69559-109 Thomas Street, Oakville, Ontario Canada L6J 7R4.
Telephone: (905) 842-4428, Facsimile: (905) 842-9327   ATTN: Mr. Reid

Trade Book Stores: Raincoast Books, 8680 Cambie Street, Vancouver, British Columbia, Canada V6P 6M9.
Telephone: (604) 323–7100, Facsimile: 604-323-2600   ATTN: Ms. Laidley

EUROPEAN UNION

England: Flex Training, Ltd. 9-15 Hitchin Street, Baldock, Hertfordshire, SG7 6A, England
Telephone: 1-462-896000, Facsimile: 1-462-892417   ATTN: Mr. Willetts

INDIA

Multi-Media HRD, Pvt., Ltd., National House, Tulloch Road, Appolo Bunder, Bombay, India 400-039
Telephone: 91-22-204-2281, Facsimile: 91-22-283-6478   ATTN: Messrs. Aggarwal

MIDDLE EAST

United Arab Emirates: Al-Mutanabbi Bookshop, PO Box 71946, Abu Dhabi
Telephone: 971-2-321-519, Facsimile: 971-2-317-706   ATTN: Mr. Salabbai

SOUTH AMERICA

Mexico: Grupo Editorial Iberoamerica, Serapio Rendon #125, Col. San Rafael, 06470 Mexico, D.F.
Telephone: 525-705-0585, Facsimile: 525-535-2009   ATTN: Señor Grepe

SOUTH AFRICA

Alternative Books, Unit A3 Sanlam Micro Industrial Park, Hammer Avenue STRYDOM Park, Randburg, 2194 South Africa
Telephone: 2711 792 7730, Facsimile: 2711 792 7787   ATTN: Mr. de Haas